THE WEEKEND CRAFTER

Stamping

THE WEEKEND CRAFTER

Stamping

Beautiful ways to decorate paper, fabric, wood, and ceramics

JULIET BAWDEN

Lark
Books

First published in the USA by
Lark Books, 50 College St., Asheville, NC 28801

Distributed by Random House, Inc., in the United States and Canada

Library of Congress Cataloging-in-Publication Data
Bawden, Juliet
    Stamping : beautiful ways to decorate paper, fabric, wood, and ceramics
in a weekend / Juliet Bawden.
        p.   cm. — (The weekend crafter)
    British ed. published in 1996 under title: Stamping in a weekend.
    Includes index.
    ISBN 1-57990-004-6 (pbk.)
    1. Rubber stamp printing.   I. Title.   II. Series.
    TT867.B38   1998
    761—dc21   97-29966
                                                              CIP

10 9 8 7 6 5 4 3 2 1

Originally published in the United Kingdom in 1996 by New Holland (Publishers) Ltd.

Copyright © 1996 New Holland (Publishers) Ltd. All rights reserved.

Editor: **Emma Callery**
Designer: **Peter Crump**
Photographer: **Shona Wood**
American adaptation: **American Pie, London and Santa Clara**
Editorial Direction: **Yvonne McFarlane**

Printed in Malaysia

All rights reserved

ISBN 1-57990-004-6

CONTENTS

INTRODUCTION

Stamping is an ideal weekend craft. You need very little in the way of equipment and it takes up little or no room. In fact, everything you need can be kept in a shoe box. It has become very popular in recent years and the paints, pens, pigments, embossing powders, and stamps available are continually increasing. This popularity means that stamps are readily available everywhere, ranging from tourist stores to toy and craft stores. However, making your own stamps has the advantages of being less expensive and quite unique. The materials from which they can be made include from sponge, foam rubber, cork, vegetables, wood, and linoleum. At the beginning of this book I will show you how to use each of these materials (see pages 8-13.)

The variety of artefacts on which to practice stamping is enormous. It ranges from interiors including walls, floors, and furniture to smaller-scale items such as boxes and other containers. You can even stamp clothing and other fabrics.

The art of stamping involves taking a block with a pattern cut into or onto it, coating it with paint, and then transferring the color and pattern onto a background. It takes a bit of practice to get the knack of how much color to apply and how hard to press the stamp. For example, you need to apply different amounts of pressure on, say, fabric as opposed to paper. Curved surfaces are more difficult, but not impossible to stamp, and stamps will slide on a shiny, glazed surface. However, a brief practice on these surfaces will soon mean that you are stamping with the best of them.

The beauty of this form of decorative paint technique is that the surfaces on which you can stamp need very little or no preparation. The only surface that may need treating is bare wood, which should be cleaned and sanded before being stamped, as with any other type of painting. The other thing to check on is that you have the right type of paint for the surface on which you are stamping — so, use fabric paints, say, on items of clothing, and latex paint on wooden furniture or other wooden items (see also page 13.) Apart from these small points, there really is nothing to stop you from starting stamping today.

From the moment that I started writing this book, any time anyone came into the work-room, they had to join in. Stamping is a completely compulsive activity, and great fun, too.

Happy stamping!

Juliet Bawden

GETTING STARTED

Simply designed stamps can be made with everyday objects. Should you want to start stamping today, find a potato, a knife, and some felt-tipped pens and make a start. However, there are many stamps with more elaborate or detailed designs which can be store-bought, giving you a wide range of styles from which to choose.

THE HISTORY OF STAMPING

Stamps and seals have been used for thousands of years. Before the twentieth century, most people were unable to read or write and so seals were a convenient way to authenticate documents or letters and indicate that their contents was important. When one person needed to communicate with another person but could not do so face to face and did not know how to write a scribe would be employed to write the document. The author would then present his seal which the scribe would impress on the material on which the missive was written. In ancient times, seals were an essential part of legal documents, business transactions, court records, and any kind of important and official writing.

Seals were distinctive and difficult to copy. Merchants would use a symbol of their trade, nobles and royalty would have special seals to mark their rank and office.

Ancient examples of seals can be seen in museums, such as a Babylonian seal dating from 4000 BC, and from 3000 BC a seal from Syria (or Ebla as it was then known.). Seals took a variety of shapes, ranging from rectangular and square to oval and circular. The round shape still remains the most popular today but in Mesopotamia and Persia. the cylindrical seals seemed to take their shape from the cuneiform writing these peoples used. The cylindrical seal was used by rolling on the tablet of wet clay used for writing, which was then allowed to dry in the sun. Sometimes these slabs of clay would then be enclosed, like the letter of today, in an envelope, but at that time, the envelope would be made from clay as well and would be sealed.

Seals and stamps have been made from a variety of materials such as clay, bone, stone, wood, ivory, and metals, and even gold or silver. They used to be placed directly on the surface of the document but later seals were impressed into softened wax. .

Seals were also embedded into rings. Most important people had their own signet rings which would be pressed into the sealing wax. This method of sealing envelopes and scrolls lasted from Roman times right up until the eighteenth and nineteenth centuries, when literacy became more widespread. Wax seals are still used on documents to give them a mark of officialdom. The Papal Bull is, in fact, a lead seal and all legal documents bear seals and stamps.

The Chinese and Japanese use seals today more frequently than most other nations, as they have done for thousands of years. This may be because the ideogram scripts lends themselves naturally to seal designs.

Modern seals and stamps are often made from rubber. Placed straight onto paper, they are used for many different purposes — in offices, libraries, and for many official tasks. In the last decade, a much greater variety of stamping equipment for decorative purposes has become available for use in the home.

This book illustrates how to make stamps from rubber, as well as from a variety of other materials such as polystyrene, linoleum, synthetic foam, fruit, torn newspaper, and sponges, as well as using more traditional wood and metal blocks.

SELECTING A MANUFACTURED STAMP

A traditional rubber stamp is made in three parts. The design (die) is cut from rubber, and this is laid onto a wooden handle (block,) with a layer of foam (cushion) sandwiched in between. When buying a rubber stamp, it is worth checking certain features to make sure the stamp is easy to use and, most importantly, that the image will be clear, once printed.

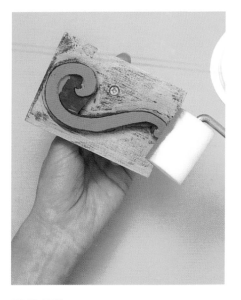

THE DIE
* Ensure that the design has been cut evenly and deeply. Designs that are too shallow will not produce a clear image, and if they are incised unevenly, the result will be that parts of the image will not appear when the stamp is used. Whatever the material used for the design, it should be trimmed as closely to the edge of the design as possible.
* Some manufacturers produce polymer stamps which enable far more intricate designs to be created. The advantage of this type of stamp is that fabric and acrylic paints are easily washed off with

water, but the slight drawback is that marker pens are not always successful.

* One other material used to make stamps is hardened plastic which can be quickly and efficiently inked. But these stamps do not allow for any highly detailed design to be inscribed.

THE BLOCK

* It is very difficult to produce a clear print just by holding onto the design, so the handle is very important. It should not be overly large as this can make it tempting to rock the stamp while printing, resulting in an uneven or smeared image.

* Blocks can be made from a variety of materials, but be wary of those made with soft materials such as foam or sponge. There might be a tendency to push down too hard which will squash both the block and the design, again causing fuzziness.

THE CUSHION

* The cushions can either be trimmed to the shape of the outline of the design or be the same shape as the handle. When pressure is applied, check that it is only the design that touches the surface, and not the lower edge of the handle. The depth of the cushion should therefore be checked before buying or making a stamp.

MOUNTING ADHESIVE

* The three parts of the stamp are held together with adhesive which is usually a rubber cement or a mounting film. Inks are solvent-based and so they will eventually destroy the adhesive used to stick the parts of the stamp together, so it is very important to clean the stamps thoroughly after use. Water-based products, such as some marker pens, cannot do any damage.

CARE OF STAMPS

1 To ensure that the die stays in good condition, always store all stamps with their rubber side downward.
2 Some inks will stain the stamp even after cleaning, especially if darker colors are used. However, as long as the stamp has been cleaned properly, this will not affect the quality of the print when the stamp is used again.
3 Stamps must be cleaned after use and when changing the color.
4 After using water-based products, stamp the pad onto a piece of scrap paper or kitchen towel, until only a vague impression is being made and then rinse under running water.
5 After using solvent-based inks, keep stamping until as little ink as possible is left — as for water-based products — and then dry them thoroughly. This should be sufficient but, if not, use a mix of water and washing-up liquid or other detergent and gently clean. You will need an old fingernail brush or toothbrush which can be used to help remove a really stubborn stain.
6 Always clean stamps immediately. When this is impossible, stamp on to a scrap piece of paper to remove as much ink as you can and then place the stamp on a damp sponge or towel. The ink that is left will not dry as long as it is kept wet.
7 When ink has dried onto the stamp, dab solvent-based cleaner onto the die and gently scrub with the fingernail brush or toothbrush.
8 Never immerse the whole stamp in water. It is quite unnecessary and could loosen the adhesive which was used to make the stamp.

TOOLS AND EQUIPMENT

You will find that you already have much of the equipment needed for making stamps and for practicing the art of stamping in your home. Many stamps, paints, inks, and materials on which to print can be store-bought, but at first, it is advisable to experiment with what is already available as this will save a lot of time and expense.

MAKING A RUBBER STAMP

For the rubber you will need:
Rubber erasers
Tracing paper
Soft pencil
Fountain pen
Needle
Craft knife
Sandpaper, Scrap paper

1 Choose an eraser of a suitable size and work out a design. A white eraser is preferable, and the less "springy" the better. For the design, either copy one of the templates from pages 76-8, or create your own pattern or picture.
2 Trace the image to be copied, or draw the design heavily onto the tracing paper using the soft pencil. Then shade on top of all the heavier drawn lines until they are covered.
3 Turn the tracing paper over and hold it firmly in place on top of the eraser.. Draw heavily on top of the lines of the design and this will then be transferred to the top of the eraser..
4 Use the fountain pen to trace over the image, correcting any missed parts. The reversed image can now be seen more clearly, so making it easier to see while cutting out.
5 Slowly stroke the needle over the outline several times, allowing the surface of the rubber to be cut just a minuscule amount. Don't score a line immediately — just stroke gently. The angle of this initial scoring should be away from the image, with no undercutting.
6 Now use the tip of a very sharp craft knife and cut the lines of the image a little deeper, taking care to keep the angle of the cut sloping. The cutaway section should narrow toward the top, like a sand dune.
7 Clean any excess ink from the eraser with a moistened tissue or baby wipe. Then place the stamp on an ink pad and take a first print onto a smooth piece of paper. You will then be able to see where rough edges need to be trimmed and to generally check that the image is correct.
8 Trim away excess rubber and any rough areas with the knife and then take another print to check. Repeat this process until a clear, satisfactory image is achieved. If there are any large areas in the design it may help to keep these clear by making deeper cuts in the eraser with the knife.
9 If small mistakes are not too deep, they can be corrected by using sandpaper to rub down the surface. If it is not possible to rectify an image, use the other side of the eraser and start again. Alternatively, if an eraser is large

enough, cut it into smaller sections, or remove one part of a design if a mistake has been made.

For the block you will need:
Wood or doweling to suit the stamp
Small saw
¼ inch-thick cellulose sponge
Adhesive

1 Cut a suitable length of wood or doweling to fit the back of the stamp. This should not overlap the stamp but it can be the same size or slightly smaller. It will be impossible to place the stamp accurately if the block is larger than the stamp, as the stamp cannot be seen if this happens.
2 Cut the cellulose sponge to the same shape as the stamp and then glue this to the back of the rubber stamp.
3 Next, glue the wooden handle to the back of the sponge.
4 Make a mark on the stamp or the handle to indicate which is the top of the image.

The stamp does not necessarily need a handle, but it is much easier to use and less messy if there is something to hold onto other than the stamp. Many offices have stamps which are no longer used, so if you can obtain some of these

the rubber can be stripped from the handle and the handle reused. Hoarded or waste objects such as thread reels, small jars with lids, and plastic boxes, can also be used as handles.

For a more professional finish, either stamp the image onto the back of the handle or onto a piece of paper which is then glued onto the handle. Give it three coats of varnish and, when dry, glue the handle onto the rubber stamp.

STAMPS MADE USING OTHER MATERIALS

As long as the stamping medium will adhere to it, you can use any object as a stamp, whatever the shape or size, plain or patterned. Thrift stores are a source of old corporate seals; metal and wooden stamps can be found at printers; cookie cutters are a useful pre-cut tool, and patterned rubber rollers from decorating and hardware stores can be used, especially if a larger area needs to be covered. Inca-wheels (roller stamps that produce a continuous pattern) can be found in craft stores nowadays, and make good presents for children as they are easy to use. They often have interchangeable wheels so you can quickly vary the designs.

CORK
Cork can be bought in sheets of varying thicknesses or you can simply use cork matting. Transfer a design onto the cork surface in the same way as above,and then, using a sharp craft knife, gradually cut out the image. Corks from bottles can also be used as stamping tools, either as circular stamps which will leave a patterned impression from the corks, or a design can be cut from the side or top, and the corks used in this way. Draw a design on the cork in pen or pencil ① and then carefully cut it out with a craft knife ②. The design should be fairly simple as cork can be difficult to cut. You can also buy more detailed cork stamps ③.

LINOLEUM

Linoleum is readily available from craft stores in standard sizes and it can be cut into different shapes with strong scissors. Draw your design directly onto the surface with a soft pencil whose marks can easily be removed with an eraser. Specialist cutting tools can be bought from craft suppliers and there are numerous different shaped blades available. These are interchangeable, so you need only purchase one handle. For information on making a lino-cut, see the lino-cut bird on pages 18-19.

Once you are happy with your design, cut around it with the cutting tool ④. Then neaten the linoleum by trimming around the stamp with a sharp pair of scissors ⑤. Cover the image with an even coat of paint ⑥, and finally stamp ⑦.

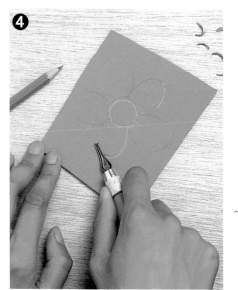

FRUITS AND VEGETABLES

Fresh produce can be used for printing with the most wonderful results. There are innumerable fruits and vegetables that can be used, such as apples, lemons, hard plums, potatoes, turnips, jicama, and carrots. When using the fruit or vegetable for its own imprint, citrus fruits and apples produce particularly interesting prints.

When cutting into the surface to create a pattern it is better to use a potato, yam, or other vegetable with a hard inner surface. Lino-cutting tools can be used for gouging out the image required and, as stated above, there are many different blades available. Dried

To cut a stamp from a piece of sponge, first draw the design onto a piece of sponge using a felt-tipped pen ⑭. Then carefully cut it out using scissors ⑮.

fruits can also be used, such as apple rings and pears ⑧. An interesting shape is particularly good for repeat patterns. To make a potato print, first clean the potato thoroughly and then cut it in half ⑨. Draw the shape onto the cut side of the potato, using a felt-tipped pen ⑩. Then, with a craft knife, cut away the part of the design you do not want printed, so that the part you want stands proud of the surface ⑪. Finally, paint color onto the part standing proud and then print onto surface ⑫.

POLYSTYRENE

Polystyrene trays used to hold fresh meats and fish sold in the supermarket make excellent surfaces from which to print. A pencil, twig, or any blunt tool can be used to make a picture or pattern on the polystyrene surface, from which a print can then be taken. This is a great idea for the kids. Children can create quite complicated patterns easily on this surface and how nice to have some use for these trays without having to throw them straight in the trash! You can also buy polystyrene or other plastic ceiling or wall tiles that are often already patterned. The pattern can be used exactly as it is ⑬.

SPONGE

Sponges come in pre-cut shapes or you can cut out the shape required from a sheet of sponge. It is easiest to use thin sponge, as thicker ones tend to be rather messy. To get a good print from sponge, it is best to apply only a thin layer of ink and not to press too hard. It is also possible to use compressed sponge, but be careful about allowing this to become wet as it will expand. It is best to mount compressed sponge on a handle.

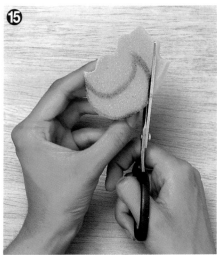

CRUMPLED PAPER

Crumpled and torn paper make interesting impressions when used as stamps. Whole walls in rooms have been printed in this way, yet at the other end of the scale, wonderful cards and wrapping papers can also be created using this method of stamping.

WOOD

Wood can be carved to make a die, though it should be noted that wooden stamps are more successful if the image stands out from the block as opposed to being indented. It is difficult to produce a clear image if it is indented because of the nature of the material.

You can buy a variety of wooden stamps from many outlets. The wooden stamps that newspaper and magazine printers used to use are often to be found in antique and junk stores.

STAMPING MEDIUM

The surface on which you are going to stamp determines the kind of ink that will be used. Most fluids can be used as inks as long as they can be applied to the die and will adhere to the material on which the stamp is to be placed. In the past, if you needed an ink-pad, you would buy one inked with a pre-selected color and once the pad was dry it could be re-inked. However, a whole variety of media can now be used and are readily available, so consult the labels on any types of ink or color to find the most appropriate product for your project.

INK

Inks can be permanent or non-permanent and this should be noted when purchasing the product. It is always easier to use a stamp-pad for these inks ① and it is possible to make one using layers of felt covered with cheesecloth. The pad should be placed in a container with a lid which will keep the pad damp, preventing the ink from drying up. Bottles of ink are available from office supply stores and art stores in a multitude of colors. The pads are best stored upside down to keep the ink at the surface.

FELT-TIPPED PENS

Felt-tipped pens are produced with permanent and non-permanent inks, water-based or solvent-based.

Experiment to find out which adheres best to which materials. The advantage of using felt-tipped pens is that different areas of the design can be colored with a variety of hues, so once stamped, a multi-colored image will appear on the surface of the material.

PAINTS

Most paints can be used for printing, whether they are powder, ink, or gouache ②. Usually, the thicker the paint, the better the result as the color will be more vibrant.

A wide range of latex paint is now available in small quantities and you can also have color customized. This type of paint produces some wonderful effects and sections of a stamp can be painted in different colors.

GENERAL TIPS BEFORE STAMPING

1 Ensure that the work surface on which you are stamping is flat and hard.

2 Make sure that all materials on which you are printing are flat. Remove creases if you are working with fabric and use masking tape to keep other products in place. This will help you to concentrate on the stamping, rather than attempting to keep the paper or fabric still as well! When stamping onto a box, lampshade, or similar item, secure the object as firmly as you can before starting to stamp.

3 Always test the stamp on a scrap of paper or fabric first, as this is the only chance you will have to rectify any problems that might occur with either the die or the medium being used.

4 Do not over-ink the stamp or the result will be a smudged image. When using an ink-pad, lightly tap the stamp on the surface, do not press down hard. If using a brush to apply paint, make sure it has been gently stroked along the edge of the pot before brushing onto the image and ensure that the paint is applied evenly. It is worth noting that less ink is needed when the image is finely detailed.

5 Do not "rock" the stamp once on the surface as the image will blur. Larger stamps need firm pressure at the center and while held in place; lighter pressure should be applied around the edges.

6 If you are using a second color over an initial stamped design, always allow plenty of time for the first impression to dry.

GIFTS FOR THE HOME

Gifts for the home include both utilitarian and decorative objects. This is the place to look for ideas for housewarming presents, or just a gift to say thank you when you have been a weekend guest. Even something as simple as a bar of soap can be made into a special gift by wrapping it in plain brown paper and stamping a design on the paper. Flowerpots are inexpensive and can be easily stamped with a decoration. Choose a color that complements the decor and buy or create a design that you know the recipient of your gift will like.

CERAMIC DAISY-STAMPED VASE

A simple, dark blue ceramic vase looks as if it might be the easiest thing one could possibly stamp. However, on a curved and shiny surface, it can be difficult to stamp your image without it slipping about. The only advice for achieving the perfect stamp, is to practice before you try stamping your chosen piece. Or incorporate the sliding of the stamp and the imperfections into a pattern, layering the stamps one over another, as has been done here.

1 Making sure that the stamp is clean and dry, use the paintbrush to smoothly paint the entire stamp white. It is best to start at the center of the stamp and work outward to the edges.

VARIATIONS

Try alternating the colors of the flowers so that some of them are printed white on yellow; or how about just stamping the flowers around the rim of the pot?

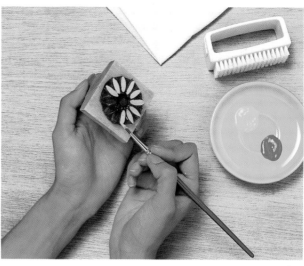

2 Place the stamp on the vase, press down firmly, and roll across the surface so that the whole image is transferred to the vase. Paint the stamp white again and repeat to cover the vase randomly in white daisies. Leave to dry.

3 Wash off the paint in warm water, using a fiingernail brush or toothbrush to ensure all the crevices are clean; pat dry with a clean cloth and then paint only the petals of the daisy stamp with the yellow latex paint.

4 Stamp over the white daisies that are already there, so that the white shows through and the petals are yellow and white. Repeat to cover all the white flowers on the vase.

5 Clean off the stamp again, paint only the center of the flower with the red latex paint and then stamp it into the center of each daisy. Remember that it doesn't matter if the stamp slips slightly, as these imperfections can be incorporated into the pattern.

WOODEN CHAIR WITH BIRD LINOLEUM PRINTS

Linoleum cuts make unique stamps; the design can be your own or copied from something that you like. The cutting made for this chair is of a little bird, which was cut to fit onto the width of the wooden slats. The effect from linoleum stamps is quite rough as the image is transferred unevenly, but it can be touched up if you prefer a smooth finish.

1 Remembering that the lines you draw will be in relief once they are stamped. Draw a design onto the linoleum with your marker pen or pencil. The simpler your design, the stronger the stamped image will be. If you want to use the same bird design, transfer the template on page 77 onto the lino.

YOU WILL NEED

Small piece of linoleum

Fine marker pen (black) or a soft pencil

Bird template (page 77)

Linoleum cutter

Scissors or craft knife

Wooden chair

Paintbrush (fine)

Stamping paint (stone color)

— VARIATIONS —

You will see from the photograph on the left, that birds have also been stamped onto the seat of this slatted chair. Instead of repeating this triangular pattern, perhaps you could randomly scatter the birds across the seat, or make an arrow-head shape, as if for a flock of birds in flight.

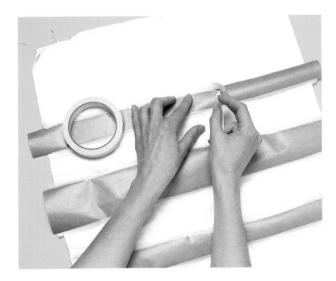

2 Cut two equal-sized pieces from the cotton fabric. Next, place the paper onto one of the pieces (the pillow front) at equal distances apart and tape down the paper with the torn masking tape. Make sure that the torn edges face outward onto the fabric. Don't feel that the lines have to be accurately straight; some variation in the lines adds to the textural interest of this pillow.

3 Pour small quantities of the black and white fabric paints into the plastic container, allowing them to mix slightly where the paints meet. Then take the household sponge and cover the surface evenly with the two paints, stamping off any excess onto scrap paper.

4 Stamp along the spaces on the pillow cover created by the paper and tape. As you apply more paint to the sponge, you will find that the black will slowly change to charcoal and then to gray as the black and the white mix together. Make the most of this by going over some of the darker areas where the paint has become lighter, or use the part of the sponge that has more white on it. Repeat the stamping until all the exposed fabric has been covered.

5 Leave the paint to dry and then slowly remove the tape and the newspaper to reveal the pattern beneath. If you want the back of your pillow to look the same as the front, repeat these steps on the second piece of fabric. To fix the paint, iron the fabric on the reverse side with a medium-hot iron. Then make up the cover. With right sides facing, stitch around three edges with a ½-inch seam allowance. Insert a pillow pad and then neatly oversew the last seam to close the gap.

GIFTS FOR THE HOME GALLERY

Flowerpot
Ceramic is a difficult surface on which to stamp. It is easier to stamp onto unglazed pottery, as the stamp will not slide. On curved surfaces such as these, start with one side of the stamp and roll it over the surface and lift in one deft movement.

Soaps
Soap can be turned into a special gift by wrapping in plain brown, green, and blue paper and stamping with a shell design.

Tiles
Bathroom tiles can either be stamped using alkyd paint or with latex paint which is then given a protective coat of varnish.

Gift box
A small plywood box has the center of a tile stamped onto its lid and a tiny pattern stamped round its sides.

Table mats

Easy-to-make table mats made from fringed burlap stamped in two shades of terracotta.

Lampshade

A shabby lampshade has been given a new lease of life by sponging with mushroom-colored latex paint, and leaving it to dry before sponging gold sea horses around the edge.

Saucer

Unglazed ceramic takes stamps very successfully – this saucer is stamped with daisy sections.

Picture frame

A wooden frame has been given a color wash before being stamped with linoleum cuts of stars and flashes.

Pitcher

A small pitcher is stamped on its unglazed surface using white quarter daisies with yellow centers.

2 Stamp the design onto the paper template to see how it will look on the pot. If you do not like the pattern, you can try something else on another collar without making a mess of the flowerpot. If you are changing colors on the block, wash off the paint in warm water, using a fingernail brush to ensure all the crevices are clean; pat dry with a clean cloth and then reapply paints and try out the design once more.

3 Apply more paint to the block and, holding it firmly against the flowerpot, roll it from one side to the other without lifting it from the surface of the pot. Now lift off the stamp, being careful not to smudge the paint.

4 Turn the block through 180 degrees so that the pattern is turned around, add more paint, and repeat step 3. Continue in this way, adding more paint to the block as you go, until the base of the flowerpot is covered with the design. If necessary, neaten the stamp prints with the paintbrush.

5 For the top rims, paint just a small portion of the stamp and make a pattern around the top edge of the flowerpot to make a border. Stamp a complete daisy on the base of the pot, too, if you wish.

SWIRLY STAMPED WINDOW BOX

If you know what color flowers you will be putting into your window box, you can choose to stamp it with complementary colors. A nice idea is to use the same stamp throughout and change the colors as you go along. Come summertime, you will have a profusion of glorious colors filling your window ledge.

VARIATIONS

For a seaside box, paint it all over with a pale blue wash and use the same image in dark blue, but across the panels to form overlapping waves. Alternatively, fall leaves motif box can be created by stamping leaves in browns, ochers, and yellows.

1 Using the roller, cover the surface of the swirl stamp evenly with pink latex paint. It is easier to get an even coverage on a larger stamp like this one by using a roller. Pour some of the paint into a plastic tray or a saucer and roll the roller through the paint, ensuring an even coverage.

2 Press the stamp down firmly onto the first slat of the window box, pressing the stamp to make sure that the entire image has been transferred. Then lift the stamp off swiftly to avoid smudging. Repeat the same stamping operation on every third slat.

3 Using the damp cloth or sponge, clean off the stamp meticulously. Use the fingernail brush to ensure you get every last bit of paint off of the stamp. Then cover the stamp with the green latex paint and stamp on the second slat. Repeat on every third slat after that.

4 Clean off the stamp, again, and this time cover the stamp evenly with yellow paint ready to stamp on the remaining slats. To finish off the box, paint the top and bottom grooves with white latex, as in the photograph opposite. Sand down any uneven edges when the paint is dry.

CONTAINERS GALLERY

Busy bees
A small round box is painted in turquoise latex paint and then stamped with bees in contrasting yellow.

Shoe boxes
These are great for storing lots of items. Paint them white to cover up the labels before painting bright colors over the top and decorating them with linoleum prints.

Seed packet container
Needing to find a box to store all those half-used packets of seeds, I came upon the perfect answer – a boring brown cardboard box. I gave it a new lease of life with some red paint and a carrot stamp.

Shaker boxes
These boxes have been painted fuchsia pink and then stamped with the traditional Shaker symbol of the hand and heart.

Trash basket

This trash basket is made from cardboard and has been painted bright yellow on the outside, then a large spot design has been stamped on it in red, using the foam-covered lid from a box of dressmaking pins. The colors are reversed on the inside of the basket.

Serving tray

The brightly contrasting orange and green paints on this tray have a modern-looking cactus design stamped on the lid.

STATIONERY

Whether it is writing paper, envelopes, or gift tags, stationery can be decorated to great advantage using stamps. Children's stationery can be made by using pretty stamps in bright colors. A border is effective on a piece of writing-paper, and a single motif on the back of an envelope is rather attractive. Plain, inexpensive stationery can be uplifted and made special by using a stamp, and, sometimes, old printer's blocks can be found and used as modern stamps. If you can find letters you can then stamp your own initials on your stationery. Stamp on plain adhesive labels to make book plates, or make decorative labels for jelly jars of home preserves.

FLEUR-DE-LYS BOX FILE

The fleur-de-lys is a very popular and striking image, especially for the festive season. Here it is used with black latex and white acrylic paints to give an otherwise plain cardboard box file a touch of class.

1 Open the flat box file right out and cover it completely with the black latex paint. Allow the first coat to dry and then paint on a second. Leave this one to dry too.

VARIATIONS

This fleur-de-lys stamp is store-bought; there are a wide range of different designs available. But why don't you cut your own out of a potato, cork, or sponge (see pages 10-12) so that your file is unique?

2 To mark out the box to position the stamps, first measure the width of the stamp with a ruler, and then measure along the base edges of the box file. With the pencil, mark off how many stamps will fit along the edge. On this particular file, three fleur-de-lys images fitted along each side and one was centered neatly on the back.

3 Using the fine paintbrush and white acrylic paint, cover the stamp surface as evenly as possible. Too much paint on one area will result in an uneven print being made when it comes to the stamping.

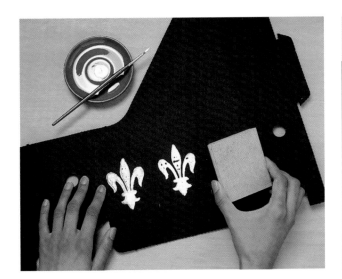

4 Stamp down the fleur-de-lys firmly where you have marked off the spaces. A box file like this is made of corrugated cardboard, making the surface slightly springy, so ensure that you press down very firmly, and at the same time rock the stamp to and fro. Repeat until you have completed your pattern, painting on more paint between each stamp.

5 Because of the uneven surface of corrugated cardboard, you may find the stamps are uneven. If necessary, now is the time to touch up the fleur-de-lys, using the white acrylic paint and fine paintbrush.

DAISY ENVELOPES

Customize and personalize your own and your child's stationery by stamping small prints onto paper and envelopes alike. The designs can range from tiny black prints on white writing paper to brightly colored daisies, like those on the envelopes stamped here.

YOU WILL NEED

Daisy stamp

Acrylic paints (pink, green)

Paintbrush (fine)

Plain envelopes

VARIATIONS

On the writing paper, a border has been stamped all the way around, but it would be just as interesting to stamp down just one side, say, or along the bottom edge. The end result would be nicely understated.

1 Holding the daisy stamp steady, carefully paint the petals using the pink acrylic paint. Use the fine paintbrush to do this, as it means you will be less likely to smudge the paint.

2 Clean the paintbrush in warm water and then paint the center of the flower with the green acrylic paint. Make sure that the paint is the right thickness for stamping by testing the stamp on scrap paper first.

3 Decide on where you wish to stamp the daisy and press the stamp down firmly, rocking it ever so slightly from side to side to ensure that the whole image is transferred. Lift the stamp swiftly and in one smooth movement to avoid smudging.

4 You may find that the stamped image is uneven in places. If so, paint over any part of the petals or the center that you wish to tidy up with the same paintbrush.

POTATO-PRINTED WRAPPING PAPER

Creating a stunning gift wrap paper is easier than it seems: this paper started life as plain brown packaging paper and a potato. Potato prints allow you to carve your own stamp designs, making your stamps unique and individual. However, remember that the simpler your design, the bolder your stamped image will be.

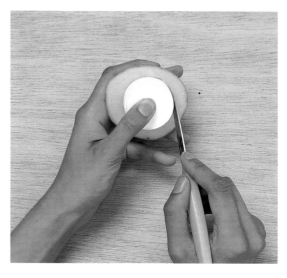

1 Cut a potato in half lengthwise, so that you get the largest possible surface on which to carve your design. Take just one half of the potato, and place the circular object onto it to use as a template. A small jar lid is ideal for this purpose. Then use the sharp knife to cut around the lid carefully. Cut about ½ inch, deep making sure not to cut straight through the potato.

YOU WILL NEED

Large potato

Sharp knife

Round object to use as a template, such as a lid

Kitchen paper

Stamping paint (cream-colored)

Paintbrush (fine)

Brown packaging paper

VARIATIONS

Don't feel obliged to stick with one color for the stamps on wrapping paper. Alternate colors across the rows, or just mix them up any old how. Bright gouache paints can be mixed into a whole rainbow of colors.

2 To make the circle stand proud, carefully trim away the excess potato. Use the same knife and slowly slice around the potato paring off the pieces of potato that lie outside the circle.

3 Before applying the paint, pat the potato dry on a piece of kitchen paper. Then paint the potato stamp with the stamping paint, applying the paint quite thickly with the paintbrush.

4 Place the stamp onto the brown packaging paper and press down firmly, taking care not to let the stamp slide or slip. To avoid smudging the paint, lift the stamp off in one movement.

5 Repeat the stamping like this until you achieve the pattern that you desire adding more paint to the potato between each stamp. The pattern made here is created by stamping the circles in lines across the paper, until the paper is full.

STATIONERY GALLERY

Writing paper and envelopes
By purchasing relatively inexpensive writing paper and envelopes and printing a border design, a designer look can be achieved for next-to-nothing.

Notepaper
The leaf design used on the recycled notepaper and envelopes is a modern polymer block.

Gift tags
A hole-punch, some string, and a single stamp make personalized gift tags.

Birthday cards
It can be difficult to find just the right card for someone. The design here is for a Pisces friend. It is a simple lino-cut, printed in one color.

Storage drawer unit

A boring cardboard drawer unit has great appeal when it is painted and stamped with a pair of retro 1950s-style Grace Kelly sunglasses.

Gift boxes

The little black-and-white gift boxes are stamped with a single motif on each side. They are great for tiny presents.

GIFTS FOR CHILDREN

Children like stamped images and they also love to stamp. Any items, from furniture to friezes, can be stamped, including toy-boxes, toys, and tee-shirts. Children's toy stores sell ready-made stamps in rubber which often come in kit form with a handle and base, into which different stamps may be fixed. Likewise, toy departments sell cut shapes in sponge which may be used for stamping on larger items such as walls or furniture. When stamping for children you are likely to find, as I did, that you are stamping with the children! This craft is so easy, everyone wants to join in.

CORK-STAMPED LAMP

A cork is a very simple and effective way of stamping, giving an unsophisticated and yet attractive look to the stamped image. The lamp and base here are stamped in contrasting red and white.

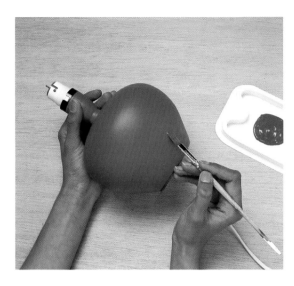

1 Remove the shade from the base and then paint the lamp base with three or four coats of the red latex paint. This many coats gives a smooth and even color to the base. Allow the paint to dry between the layers.

VARIATIONS

Don't paint the lamp base red, keep it white and stamp it with the same color as the lampshade, or stamp the shade and base with two different colors, but both on white backgrounds.

2 Take one of the corks and paint the end with the same red latex that you have just been using. You might need to put on quite a lot of paint to begin with, as it will initially soak into the cork.

3 Placing one hand on the back of the surface on which you are working so as to support the shade, press the paint-covered cork onto the shade. To ensure a complete shape when the cork is removed, rotate the wrist that is holding the cork.

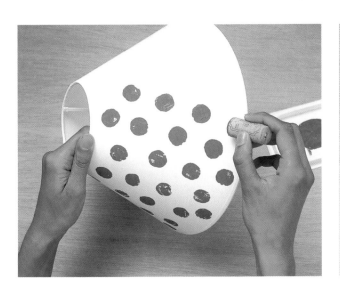

4 Repeat this step randomly all over the shade, painting the cork at every second or third stamp. Rather than working around the shade in rows, it is easiest to work from the top to the bottom on each portion as this means you don't have to keep on turning the shade around all the time.

5 Paint the second cork with the white latex and stamp the base in the same manner as you did the shade. To give a smoother finish, touch up the stamps on the base with white latex paint and a paintbrush. The cork stamps on the shade, however, actually look better when they are left to look natural.

GALLOPING HORSES RIBBON

All little girls love horses and they also love to wear ribbons in their hair. To stamp images onto ribbon is very simple, although the kind of ribbon you use is important. The recommended ribbon to stamp onto is the translucent ribbon used here or a single-backed satin ribbon. On double-backed ribbon a stamped image tends to bleed so it is best to avoid this.

1 Take a length of ribbon, then by measuring the length of the stamp and how many stamps you require on the ribbon cut it to the right size. Press using the iron set at a medium temperature.

YOU WILL NEED

Length of translucent ribbon (cream-colored)

Pencil

Ruler

Sharp scissors

Iron

Galloping horses stamp

Stamping ink pad (plum)

⚠️

SAFETY NOTE
If you are stamping ribbons for very young children, ensure that the paints you use are non-toxic.

VARIATIONS
Group the horses together so that there is a space between each "herd." Or have brown, black, and white horses galloping across the ribbon.

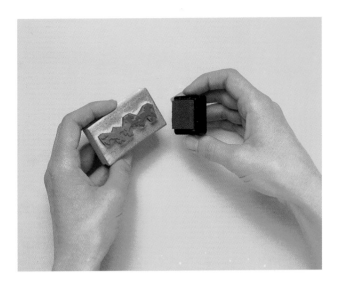

2 Apply the stamping ink to the galloping horses stamp, by either tapping the stamp onto the ink-pad or by wiping the ink-pad over the stamp. Make sure the ink is applied evenly all over the stamp.

3 Place the stamp onto the ribbon and press it down firmly, rocking it slightly from side-to side to ensure that the whole image is transferred onto the ribbon. Some of the ink may pass through the ribbon, so protect your work surface with a layer of newspaper or sheet of cardboard.

4 Continue to stamp the horses along the ribbon placing each subsequent stamp at the end of the previously completed one. For a consistently-colored ribbon, put on more ink for each stamp; for some variation, stamp two or three images before adding more ink.

5 To finish off the ribbon neatly and to prevent fraying, take each end of the ribbon and use the scissors to snip out a triangle so that there is a "V" at each end. For a simpler end, just cut off some of the ribbon at an angle.

PLANES AND CLOUDS STORAGE UNIT

Sponge shapes are available in toy stores and they make great stamps. Unlike more conventional sponging, however, you need to press down on the sponge quite firmly. In this way, you make sure that the shape doesn't smudge, and that there is a definite image with a sharp outline when the sponge is lifted.

1 Paint the cabinet with a base coat of white latex paint, using the wider paintbrush. Leave the paint to dry, wash out the paintbrush thoroughly, and then apply two coats of the bright yellow latex paint.

YOU WILL NEED

Bedside cabinet or storage unit

Latex paints (white, yellow)

Household paintbrush 2 inches wide

Artist's paintbrushes, 1 fairly thick, 1 fine

Sponge lid from a pin-box, or a round piece of sponge

Acrylic paints (white, blue)

Airplane-shaped sponge

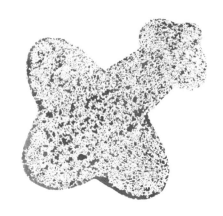

VARIATIONS

Add decorations to the airplanes once the stamps have dried. Some could have dots added to them, others wavy lines, each in strong, contrasting colors.

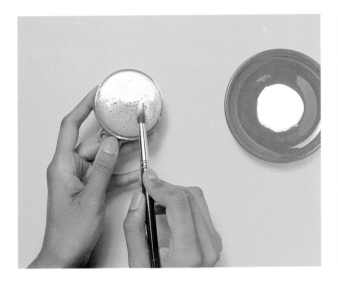

2 To make the clouds, paint the round sponge quite thickly with the white acrylic paint, applying the paint with the artist's paintbrush. Pat off excess paint onto a piece of scrap paper, and then apply the paint to the storage unit.

3 Pat down the sponge gently so that the stamped image is soft, with no definite lines, and make the cloud-shape by stamping the sponge images in a clockwise direction. Fill in the center after you have finished the surround.

4 Wash the artist's paintbrush thoroughly and then paint the airplane-shaped sponge with the blue acrylic paint. Stamp it onto the unit randomly, making sure that the transferred images are sharp. If they aren't, touch them up with the fine paintbrush.

5 Wash the sturdy paintbrush thoroughly once again and then use the round sponge and the white acrylic paint once more to stamp cloud trails behind the plane shapes to finish off.

GINGHAM BAG

Gingham fabric comes in bright, cheerful colors — predominantly blue, red, and yellow — and it is the ideal fabric for a child's bedroom, whether for curtains, a throw, or, as here, a handy bag for putting things in. The red star stamped all over it adds a very attractive decoration.

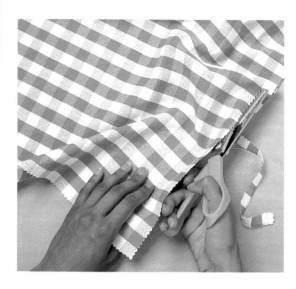

1 Cut a piece of gingham to the width of the finished bag plus 2 inches seam allowances, and twice the desired length. Press the fabric so that it is smooth when being stamped on.

YOU WILL NEED

Gingham fabric

Dressmaker's scissors

Pencil

Star stamp

Paintbrush

Fabric paint (red)

Cotton thread

Ribbon

VARIATIONS

Make stars of all colors — don't feel obliged to stick to one color, like here. Alternatively, stamp onto every white square but in alternate rows, leaving every other row blank.

2 To prevent confusion when printing, mark every square with a faint pencil dot where you are going to print. Do this on the right side of the fabric and then lay out the fabric ready to be stamped on.

3 Paint the fabric paint onto the motif, using the paintbrush. Then place the motif above the first square where you wish the color to be dark and carefully apply it.

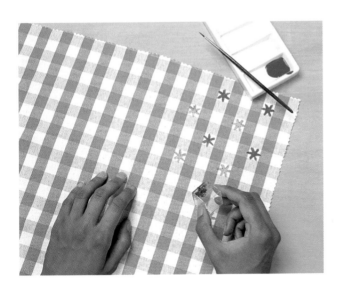

4 Without repainting the motif, stamp it into the next square. In this way you will get a pattern of light and dark motifs. Continue stamping the star across the bag in the same way.

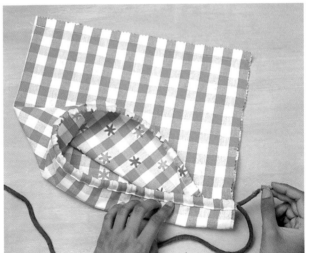

5 Make up the bag by folding it in half with the right sides together and the fold at the bottom of the bag. Then sew up the sides with a neat running stitch. At the top of the bag make a casing for the ribbon by folding over the top twice and stitching it in place, leaving a gap for the ribbon to be inserted. Thread the ribbon through to finish the bag — use a safety pin at the end to help it — and finally turn the right sides out.

GIFTS FOR CHILDREN GALLERY

Tulip frieze
Wall-friezes can be expensive, bu
this one wasn't. It was made b
cutting lining paper, painting
with latex paint, and stamping on
design made on cut potatoes

Pillow cover
Potatoes were cut into simpl
geometric shapes which we
then stamped onto tickin
using bright fabri
paints. The fabric wa
then made int
pillow cover

Child's chair
Painted bright blue, the chair has been stamped
with a lino cut tiny star, a polymer medium star,
and a sponge cheese-textured crescent moon.

Roller shade

This large flat surface is crying out to be personalized, and so a star has been stamped in two colors to complement the color scheme in a child's room.

Papier mâché clock

Painted in green and yellow, this clock has had its hands painted red and stamp designs have been used instead of numerals to make the clock face.

Tee-shirt

Small fruit stamps enliven the plainest tee-shirt very simply.

A child's storage box

A miniature chest of drawers stamped with a daisy design.

57

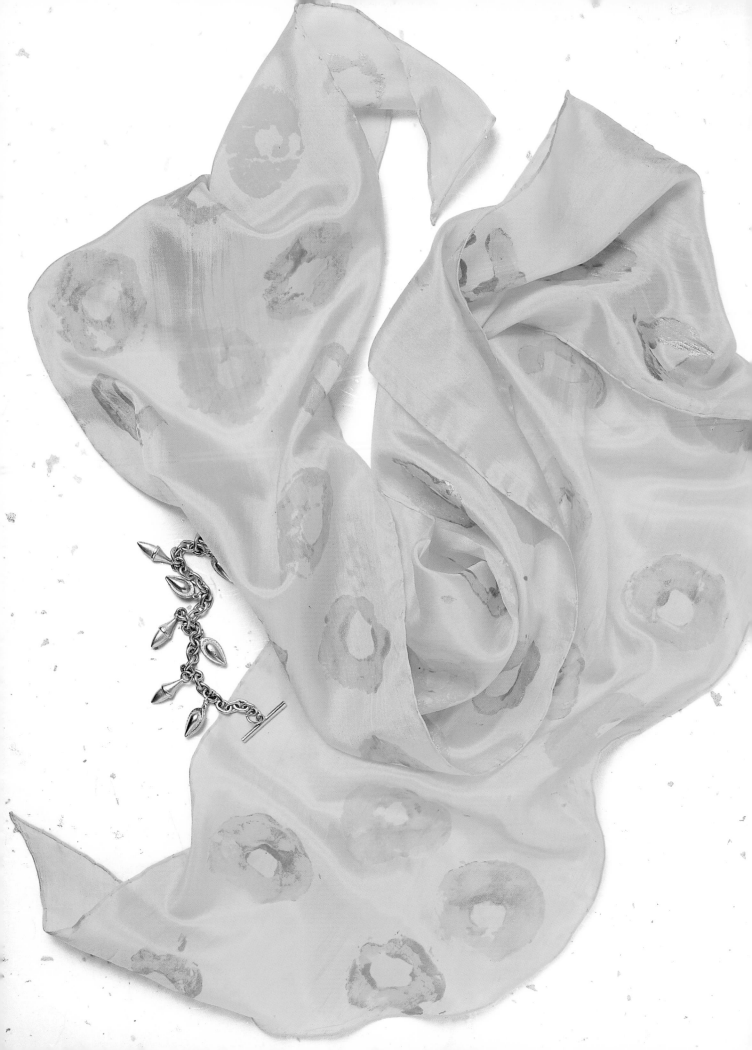

GIFTS FOR ADULTS

*T*he items in this chapter are personal ones that
you might make for yourself or would like to give as
a gift. We have included clothing such as shoes and
a scarf. The scarf was printed using a dried apple
ring; a picture album was stamped using a simple
wooden block imported from India, and a notebook
for gardeners personalized by stamping on garden
implements. If you cannot get hold of the exact
stamps we have used, make your own by cutting
linoleum or vegetables to make a print (see pages
11-12.) By stamping your personality onto a gift
you are making an object to be cherished.

FISH PHOTOGRAPH ALBUM

On the recycled cover of this photograph album, a hand-carved wooden stamp has been used repeatedly to create an effective pattern in monochrome.

1 Measure how long the fish stamp is and work out how many times it will fit across the cover so that you can plan your pattern. Carefully mark off the positions of the stamp with the pencil and ruler.

YOU WILL NEED

Photograph album with a plain recycled cover

Pencil

Ruler

Eraser

Wood-cut fish stamp

Stamping inks (black, white)

Paintbrush (fine)

Fingernail brush

— VARIATIONS —

Instead of having the fishes swimming neatly in rows across the front of this photograph album, perhaps they could be swimming in shoals, or a group of them following a lone fish somewhere out front. The beauty of stamping is that you can be very free-and-easy with your design ideas. It is always worth experimenting on scraps of paper beforehand.

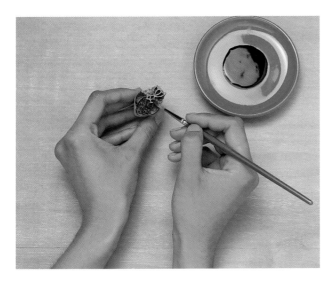

2 Paint the fish stamp with the black stamping paint, using the fine paintbrush. Before printing with the stamp, check that there are no air bubbles visible; these will make the stamps uneven.

3 Stamp the fish onto the cover where you have marked off. Press down the stamp firmly to ensure a solid outline and lift directly off the paper to avoid smudging.

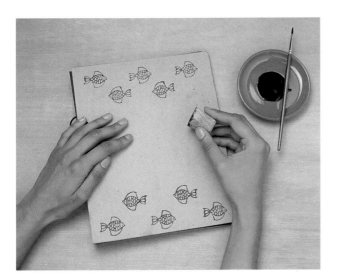

4 Repeat stamping the fish until the pattern you require has been achieved. Add more paint to the stamp each time, to ensure that you make consistent prints across the photograph album.

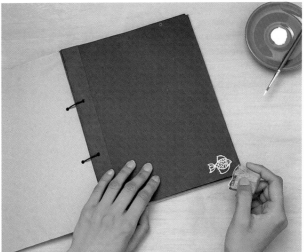

5 Clean the stamp and paintbrush thoroughly. It is best to do this by rinsing them out under a running faucet, scrubbing the stamp with the fingernail brush. Once you have dried off the stamp, paint it white, and then stamp the lower right-hand corner of each page, allowing each page to dry before turning onto the next.

CORK TABLE MATS

Just as cork is a simple medium to use for stamping, it is excellent for receiving a stamped design. Cork table mats are crying out to be stamped upon and with this simple string method, you can create all sorts of different designs.

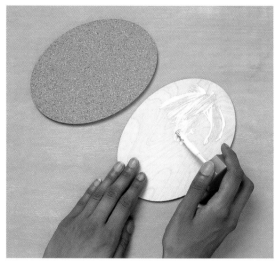

1 Cut a shape from the cardboard to exactly the same size as the cork mat. Simply place the mat on the cardboard, draw around it with a pencil, and then cut. If you are using plywood, draw around the mat and then stick the string down within this outline. Unless you have a jigsaw to hand, there is no need to cut out the shape. Cover the cardboard in glue.

YOU WILL NEED

Cork mats
Cardboard or plywood
Pencil
Scissors
Glue
String
Latex paint (black)
Paintbrush
Varnish (gloss or matt)

— VARIATIONS —

All manner of patterns can be made with the string, ranging from zigzags to Greek keys. For a design that needs to be regularly spaced, it is best to draw the pattern onto the cardboard with a pencil before sticking the string in place. In this way, you can easily make changes by erasing and starting again.

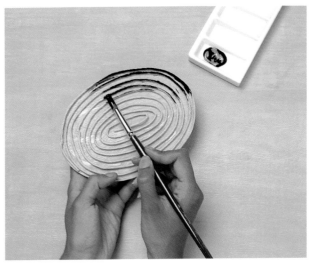

2 Stick down the string in one long spiral onto the printing board. Press it down firmly so that the string is stuck to the board very well and then leave the board to dry.

3 Apply the latex paint to the string, using the paintbrush. Use only small quantities of paint at a time, so that it doesn't fill up the spaces between the string too much.

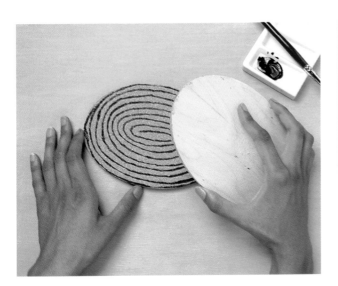

4 Place the stringed board on top of the cork mat and then press it firmly down all over. Lift the board off and a string image will be transferred to the mat. For each further mat that you are going to stamp, repaint the string, to retain a good, strong image.

5 To finish off each mat, paint the edges with the same color. Then leave to dry and paint on several coats of varnish to act as a sealant. Leave each coat to dry before adding the next one.

GIFTS FOR ADULTS GALLERY

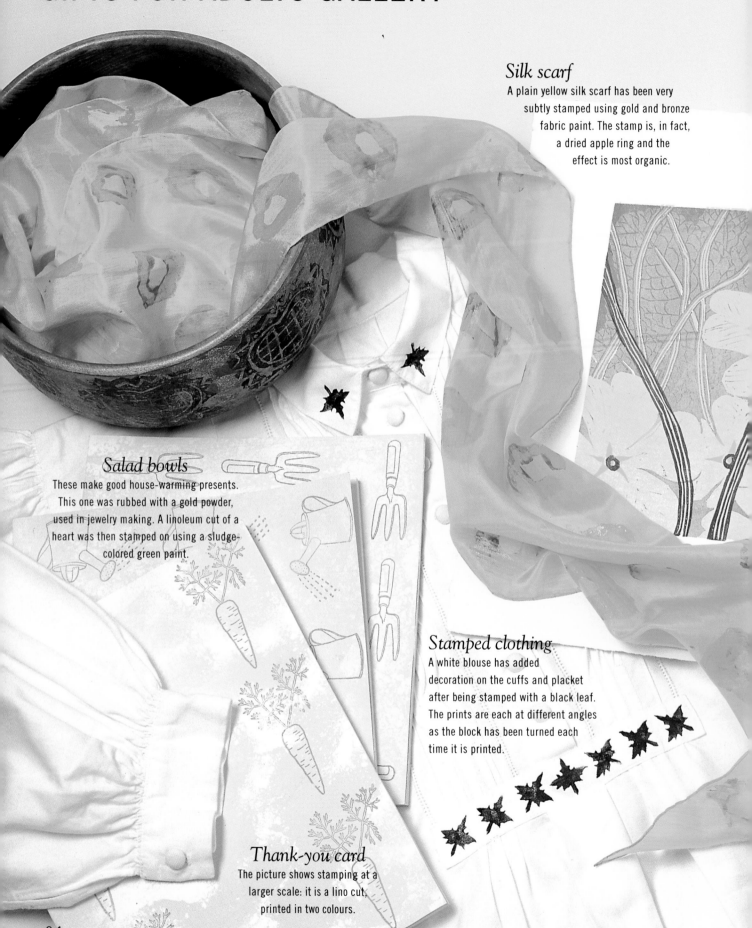

Silk scarf
A plain yellow silk scarf has been very subtly stamped using gold and bronze fabric paint. The stamp is, in fact, a dried apple ring and the effect is most organic.

Salad bowls
These make good house-warming presents. This one was rubbed with a gold powder, used in jewelry making. A linoleum cut of a heart was then stamped on using a sludge-colored green paint.

Stamped clothing
A white blouse has added decoration on the cuffs and placket after being stamped with a black leaf. The prints are each at different angles as the block has been turned each time it is printed.

Thank-you card
The picture shows stamping at a larger scale: it is a lino cut, printed in two colours.

Folk art cabinet
The design on the cabinet of folk-art birds and hearts has been created by building up the design using a variety of different stamps.

Stamped shoes
Rather dull brown suede espadrilles have been decorated for a beach holiday with a stamp of a large sea shell.

Paper lampshade
The fleur-de-lys is a popular motif and it has been used here with great effect on a paper lampshade.

65

2 Carefully cut out the design using the craft knife. Cut around the edges first and then carefully cut out slithers of rutabaga from the more detailed parts, such as the eyes and mouth.

3 Cut the lining paper to the depth you would like the frieze to be, and paint it orange. To achieve the above paint effect, load the paintbrush with paint and then dip it in some water before transferring it to the shelf paper. In this way, the degrees of color intensity will vary. Leave the paint to dry.

4 First stamp on the pumpkin images. Using the black paint, paint the pumpkin face on the swede and then stamp along the frieze. Add paint to the swede between each stamp to retain a consistent printed image.

5 Using black paint again, stamp the bats onto the frieze. Position them between, above and below the pumpkin faces and let them fly at different angles by rotating the swede as you stamp.

EMBOSSED CHRISTMAS DECORATIONS

Embossing is a stamping technique with an amazing result. Here, for a festive feel, Christmas decorations are made by embossing cartridge paper with copper and silver powder. They are then cut out to make small shapes suitable for hanging from a tree.

1 Using the black ink pad and either the fleur-de-lys or paisley stamps (here, we used the fleur-de-lys one), stamp the image onto the cartridge paper. Apply the ink to the stamp by tapping the stamp onto the ink pad or wiping the ink pad over the stamp.

YOU WILL NEED

Stamping ink pad (black)

Fleur-de-lys stamp

Paisley stamp

Cartridge paper

Embossing powder (copper, silver)

Paintbrush (fine)

Heat source (iron or toaster)

Scissors

Colored card

Glue

Hole punch

Ribbon

— VARIATIONS —

Make gift tags in the same way but you only need to glue a single image to the colored card so that there is space on the back for your message and name.

2 While the image is still wet, sprinkle the embossing powder (here, we used the copper powder) all over it. Shake off the excess powder onto a clean piece of paper and, if necessary, use the small paintbrush to remove any stubborn excess powder.

3 Hold the embossed construction paper above the heat source until the powder melts onto the paper. This will take a few minutes. The end result is a raised, metalic image.

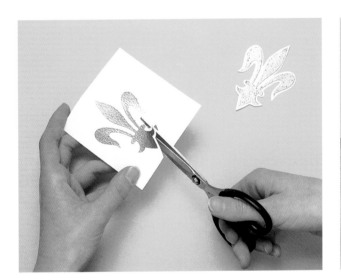

4 To make each decoration, you will need two images, one for each side, but make sure that you have a reversible design. The paisley motifs opposite would work for one-sided decorations only. Cut around each embossed image, leaving a small border, and also cut out the colored card to your required shape, remembering to allow a space at the top for a hole. Then glue the cut-out, embossed images onto both sides of the colored card and leave to dry.

5 Using the hole-punch, punch a hole in the top of the card. Then thread the ribbon through this hole, tie a knot at the top, and hang the decoration on your Christmas tree, or, say, a series of them across a window.

Wrapping paper

Red wrapping paper with a fiber running through it has been stamped with a heart design in gold. To make a pretty package it has been tied with gold and red ribbon with added hearts.

Candles

The candles have been stamped with a golden star design, using stamping paint. When stamping on wax, it is worth experimenting with different paints, as some of them will not dry but merely make a smudge.

Festive napkin holders and napkins

Suitable for parties, these can be made from cardboard tubes which are covered in a layer of papier mâché, then painted blue, and stamped with a simple gold star design. Navy paper napkins have been stamped with signs of the zodiac.

Wrapping ribbon

The ends of grosgrain ribbon have been trimmed to a point and then stamped with a heart at each end.

Voile curtain

A voile curtain is made to look special by stamping golden suns, moons, and stars all over it at random.

Pin cushion

This pin cushion was stamped with a fleur-de-lys. It makes a pretty mother's day, or birthday present. The edges of the stamped image have been dotted with pearl beads and pins.

Cracker

To make a mother's day wrapping paper, a rose design was cut from linoleum and stamped on green paper. The present was then wrapped up to look like a bonbon.

Candle shades

These have been stamped with a repeat paisley design which fits perfectly.

TEMPLATES

Linoleum stamps have been used in various projects throughout the book. To make your own lino prints like these, use a photocopier to enlarge or reduce the images as required. Place a piece of carbon paper, ink side down, on to a piece of linoleum and then place the photocopied image on top of the carbon paper. Trace over the photocopied image and through the carbon paper with a pen or pencil. Remove the carbon paper and photocopied image to reveal a carbon copy of your image. Using a pen, go over the image on the linoleum to give a clearer idea of where to cut. Take a linoleum cutting tool and carefully cut out the image on the linoleum. Follow instructions for making a stamp on page 11.

Festive Napkin Holder
(see page 74)

Hallowe'en Frieze
(see page 70)

Wooden Fruit Bowl
(see page 64)

Flower
(see page 11)

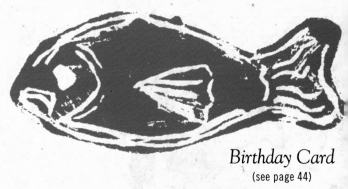

Birthday Card
(see page 44)

76

Picture Frame
(see page 28)

Child's Chair
(see page 56)

Wooden Chair with Bird
(see page 18)

Art Nouveau Rose
(see page 75)

Hallowe'en Frieze
(see page 70)

Planes and Clouds Cupboard
(see page 52)

Tulip Frieze
(see page 56)

Daisy Vase
(see page 16)

Valentine Card
(see page 68)

Tulip Frieze
(see page 56)

INDEX